36 Solos for Young Singers

Compiled by Joan Frey Boytim

To access companion recorded accompaniments online, visit
www.halleonard.com/mylibrary

Enter Code
7867-9283-6036-4978

ISBN 978-0-634-02789-5

HAL•LEONARD®
CORPORATION

7777 W. BLUEMOUND RD. P.O. BOX 13819 MILWAUKEE, WI 53213

Visit Hal Leonard Online at
www.halleonard.com

CONTENTS

8	April Fool	George H. Gartlan
10	The Blue Bells of Scotland	Traditional
12	Country Gardens	Traditional English Song
14	Cradle Song	Composer unknown (previously attributed to Wolfgang Amadeus Mozart)
5	Cuckoo	Martin Shaw
16	Dancing	Slovak Folksong arranged by Benjamin M. Culli
18	Dandelions Gold and Green	Icelandic Folksong
21	The Desperado	Traditional American Song arranged by Benjamin M. Culli
24	Didn't My Lord Deliver Daniel?	African-American Spiritual arranged by Cynthia Jackson
30	The Generous Fiddler	German Folksong arranged by Benjamin M. Culli
27	Git Along, Little Dogies	American Cowboy Song arranged by Benjamin M. Culli
32	He's Got the Whole World in His Hands	African-American Spiritual
34	Home on the Range	Traditional
36	I Know Where I'm Goin'	Irish Folksong adapted from an arrangement by Herbert Hughes
39	A Jolly Good Laugh	J. B. Thomas
42	The Keys of Heaven	Traditional English Song
44	Little David, Play on Your Harp	African-American Spiritual arranged by Harry T. Burleigh
50	Longing for Spring	Wolfgang Amadeus Mozart
47	Macnamara's Band	Shamus O'Conner

The price of this publication includes access to companion recorded accompaniments online, for download or streaming, using the unique code found on the title page. Visit **www.halleonard.com/mylibrary** and enter the access code.

52	Old Dog Tray	Stephen Foster
54	Old King Cole	16th Century English Song
56	Peace of the River	Viola Wood arranged by Benjamin M. Culli
58	The Quest	Bohemian Folk Song
60	Red River Valley	Traditional American Cowboy Song arranged by Benjamin M. Culli
62	The Sea Breeze	Folksong
64	Sidewalks of New York	Charles B. Lawlor and James W. Blake
68	Sit Down, Sister	African-American Spiritual arranged by Benjamin M. Culli
70	Skip to My Lou	19th-Century American Game Song
72	Sleep, Baby, Sleep	Folksong
73	Softly Sleeping	Franz Schubert
74	Some Folks	Stephen Foster
80	Spinning Song	German Folksong
76	Sweet and Low	Joseph Barnby
78	Tell Me Why	Traditional American Folksong arranged by Benjamin M. Culli
83	Toyland	Victor Herbert
86	The Weather	American Folksong arranged by Benjamin M.Culli

PREFACE

A current trend in many private studios and community music schools is to offer voice lessons to students who, just a few decades ago, would be considered too young for serious one-on-one vocal instruction. As more upper elementary, junior high or middle school students seek such opportunities for study, it is a challenge for teachers to find solo books with appropriate repertoire to meet the needs of these students. With those boys and girls in mind, *36 Solos for Young Singers* was compiled. Offered with a convenient companion compact disc of piano accompaniments, recorded by a professional pianist, this collection will serve as a beginning studio volume, as a collection for motivated students to explore solo singing on their own or with the help of a voice teacher, school music teacher, choir director, or simply for family fun singing sessions.

The songs include lullabies, folksongs from several nationalities, camp songs in solo arrangements, spirituals, humorous selections, and a few standards that remain popular with each new generation of singers. The majority of these solos have a range of an octave from D to D, with a few extending a note or two above or below. Most of the melodic lines are completely supported in the accompaniment, which most average pianists will find easy to play.

As you explore these 36 selections, may you find success in singing both familiar and new songs that will bring joy as you develop the art of solo singing.

Joan Frey Boytim

Cuckoo

Traditional text

Martin Shaw

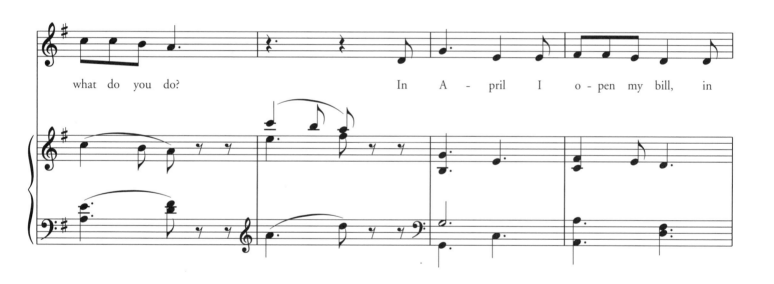

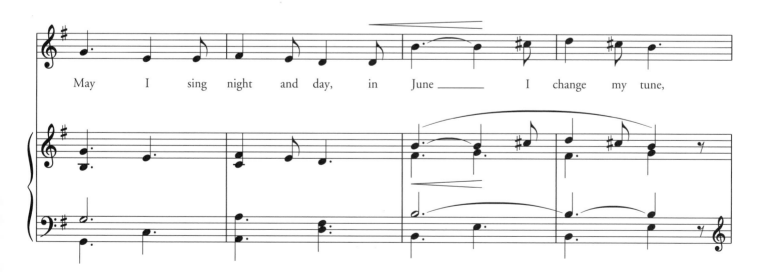

far a - way o - ver the sea, to Spain _____ I fly a - gain,

day and night I take my flight.

decresc.

Cuck - oo, good - bye _____ to

you.

poco rit.

pp

April Fool

Words and Music by
George H. Gartlan

In a spirited manner

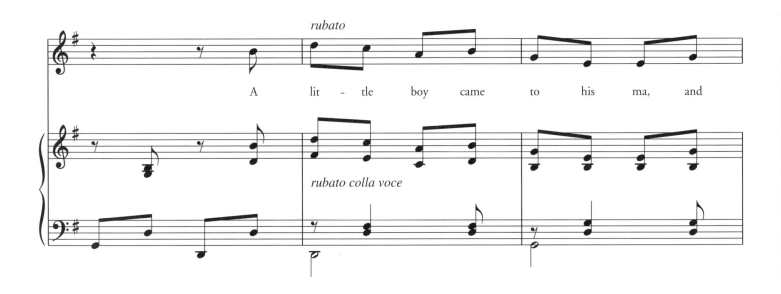

A lit - tle boy came to his ma, and

said, "I'm quite a - fraid. There's a strange man in the

The Blue Bells of Scotland

Traditional words and music

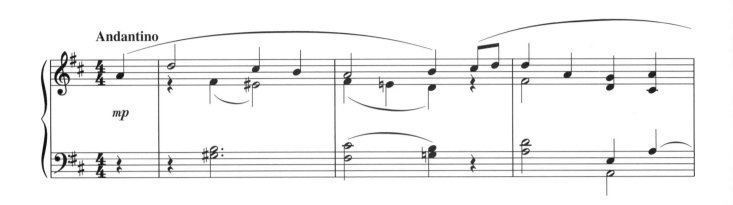

1. Oh, where, tell me where is your ___
where, tell me where did your ___

High - land lad - die gone? Oh, where, tell me
High - land lad - die dwell? Oh, where, tell me

Country Gardens

Traditional English Song

How man - y kinds of sweet flow - ers grow in an En - glish coun - try
How man - y in - sects come here and go in an En - glish coun - try
How man - y song - birds fly to and fro in an En - glish coun - try

gar - den? We'll tell you now of some that we know, those we
gar - den? We'll tell you now of some that we know, those we
gar - den? We'll tell you now of some that we know, those we

miss you'll sure - ly par - don. Daf - fo - dil, hearts - ease and phlox,
miss you'll sure - ly par - don. Fire - flies, moths and gnats and bees,
miss you'll sure - ly par - don. Bob - o - link, cuck - oo and quail,

mf

mead - ow - sweet and la - dy smocks, li - lacs, lil - ies and tall hol - ly - hocks, ros - es
spi - ders climb - ing in the trees, but - ter - flies drift in the gen - tle breeze. There are
tan - a - ger and night - in - gale, blue - bird, lark and thrush and car - di - nal. There is

p

fox - glove and snow - drops, blue for - get - me - nots, in an En - glish coun - try
snakes, ants that sting and oth - er creep - ing things in an En - glish coun - try
joy in the spring when the birds be - gin to sing in an En - glish coun - try

mf   *mp*

gar - den.
gar - den.
gar - den.

(rit. last time)

mf

Cradle Song

Composer unknown, previously attributed to
Wolfgang Amadeus Mozart

All is now qui - et and still, hushed are the vale and the hill.
All now in slum - ber doth lie, bright are the stars in the sky.

Soft be your slum - ber and deep,
An - gels a guard o'er thee keep,

sleep, oh my dar - ling, now sleep, oh sleep, _____ oh __
sleep, oh my dar - ling, now sleep, oh sleep, _____ oh __

sleep! _____
sleep! _____

Dancing

Slovak Folksong
arranged by Benjamin M. Culli

Lightly, with energy

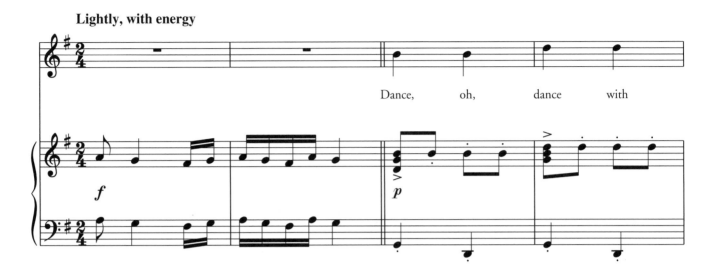

Dance, oh, dance with

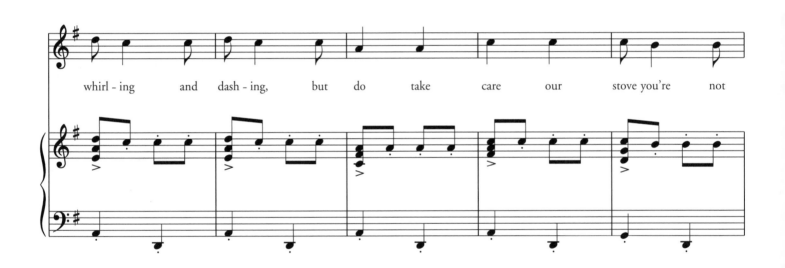

whirl - ing and dash - ing, but do take care our stove you're not

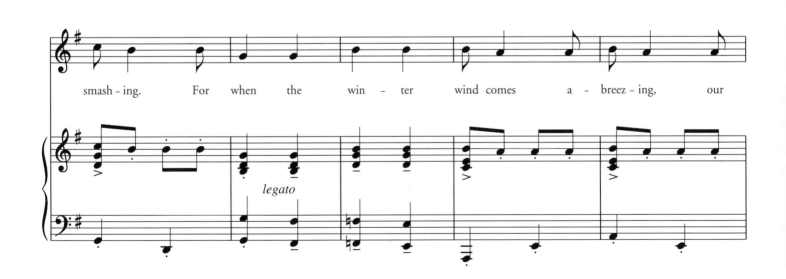

smash - ing. For when the win - ter wind comes a - breez - ing, our

Dandelions Gold and Green

Icelandic Folk Song

Dan - de - li - ons gold and green, gras - sy banks with
Dwell - er in a rock - y home, forth you come in

ber - ries grow - ing. Mead - ow sweet the wood - land queen,
might and splen - dor. Wat - er fall! I love to roam,

fair - er flow'rs have nev - er been. All the sor - row
gaz - ing at thy whirl - ing foam. Near to thee I

I have seen fades a - way _____ when the flow - ers are
love to roam, life is hap - py when love ___ is

blow - - ing. Dan - de - li - ons
ten - - der. Dwell - er in a

gold and green, grass - y banks with ber - ries grow -
rock - y home,

ing.

forth you come _____ in might and splen -

dor.

rit.

The Desperado

Traditional
arranged by Benjamin M. Culli

wore a big som-bre-ro and a gun be-neath his vest, and
got so darn ex-cit-ed that he shot out all the lights, and
grabbed him by the whis-kers, and he grabbed him by the seat, and

ev - 'ry - where he went he gave his war whoop.
ev - 'ry - where he went he gave his war whoop. } He was a
threw him where he could - n't give his war whoop.

big, brave man and a des - per - a - do, from

Crip - ple Creek way down in Col - o - ra - do, and he

Didn't My Lord Deliver Daniel?

African-American Spiritual
arranged by Cynthia Jackson

Rhythmically

Did - n't my Lord de - liv - er

Dan - iel, ___ de - liv - er Dan - iel, ___ de - liv - er Dan - iel. ___ Did - n't

my Lord de - liv - er Dan - iel ___ and why not - a ev - er - y

Git Along, Little Dogies

American Cowboy Song, 1860s
arranged by Benjamin M. Culli

As

I was a-walk-ing one morn-ing for pleas-ure I
Ear-ly in spring we round up all the dog-ies. We

saw a cow-punch-er come rid-ing a-long. His
mark 'em and brand 'em and bob off their tails. We

Pronounced tie (as in "tie your shoes") yie (same vowel sound as "tie") yoh.

The Generous Fiddler

German Folksong
arranged by Benjamin M. Culli

Who will play a
"Now, be - fore I

tune for danc - ing? Who will play ___ the fid - dle
make for you mu - sic, you will must pay ___ the fid - ler's

sweet! All the girls are shy - ly wait - ing
fee!" "Ah, we've neith - er pence nor far - thing,

He's Got the Whole World in His Hands

African-American Folksong
Possibly from North Carolina

Home on the Range

Traditional

1. Oh give me a home, where the buf - fa - lo roam, where the
of - ten at night when the heav - ens are bright with the
air is so pure the ___ zeph - yrs so free, the

deer and the an - te-lope play, ___ Where sel - dom is heard a dis-
lights from the glit - ter-ing stars, ___ have I stood there a - mazed and ___
bree - zes so balm - y and light, ___ that I would not ex - change my ___

I Know Where I'm Goin'

Irish Folksong from County Antrim
adapted from an arrangement by Herbert Hughes

I know where I'm go - in', _____ and I know who's go - in' with me.

I know who I love, but the dear knows* who I'll mar - ry!

I have stock-ings of silk, shoes of fine green leath - er,

* *"dear knows:" the Ulster equivalent of "Goodness knows."*

combs to buck-le my hair, and a ring for ev-'ry fin - ger.

cresc.

Some say he's glum, but I say he's bon - ny. The

fair - est of them all my hand-some, win-some John - ny.

Feath - er beds are soft, and paint - ed rooms are bon - ny, but

I would leave them all to __ go with my love John - ny.

I know where I'm go - in', _____ and I know who's go - in' with me. I know who I

love, _____ but the dear knows who I'll mar - ry!

cresc.

dim.

p

8vb

colla voce

p

pp

A Jolly Good Laugh

George Cooper

J.B. Thomas

laugh! Ha, ha, ha, ha, ha, ha, ha, ha, ha, ha, ha, ha, as a

jol - ly good hear - ty laugh! Ha, ha, ha, ha, ha, ha, ha, ha,

ha, ha, ha, ha, as a jol - ly good hear - ty laugh!

2. So I

The Keys of Heaven

Traditional English Song

1. I will give you the keys of ___ heav'n, I will give you the keys of ___ heav'n.
2. I will give you a blue silk ___ gown, to make you fine when you go to ___ town.
3. I will give you a coach and ___ six, six black hors - es as black as ___ pitch.
4. I will give you the keys of my heart, and we'll be mar - ried till death do us part.

Mad - am will you walk? Mad - am will you talk? Mad - am will you walk and

Verse two or three may be omitted.

Little David, Play on Your Harp

African-American Spiritual
arranged by Harry T. Burleigh

Tell ole Pha-raoh, O Lord! Loose my peo-ple, O Lit-tle Da-vid; play on your

harp, hal-le-lu, _____ Lit-tle Da-vid, play on your harp, hal-le-

lu. _____ Down in the val-ley, O Lord! I did-n't go to stay; ___

O Lord! My soul got hap-py, O Lord! An' I stayed all day, ___ O Lit-tle Da-vid,

Tempo I

play on your harp, hal - le - lu, _____ Lit - tle Da - vid, play on your

harp, hal - le - lu, _____ Lit - tle Da - vid, play on your harp, hal - le -

rit. e dim.

lu, _____ Lit - tle Da - vid, play on your harp, hal - le -

a tempo

lu. _____

McNamara's Band

John J. Stamford

Shamus O'Connor

Oh! me name is Mc - Na - ma - ra, I'm the
Now we are re - hear - sin' for a

lead - er of the band, _____ al - though we're few in
ver - y swell af - fair, _____ the an - nual cel - e -

num - ber, we're the fin - est in the land. We
bra - tion, all the gen - try will be there. When

Longing for Spring

Wolfgang Amadeus Mozart

Old Dog Tray

Stephen Foster

1. The morn of life is past, and eve-ning comes at last; it
forms I call'd my own have van-ished one by one, the
thoughts re-call the past his eyes are on me cast, I

brings me a dream of a once hap-py day, of mer-ry forms I've seen up-
lov'd ones, the dear ones have all passed a-way. Their hap-py smiles have flown, their
know that he feels what my break-ing heart would say: al-though he can-not speak I'll

on the vil-lage green, sport-ing with my old dog Tray.
gen-tle voic-es gone, I've noth-ing left but old dog Tray.
vain-ly, vain-ly seek a bet-ter friend than old dog Tray.

Old dog Tray's ev - er faith - ful; grief can - not drive him a -

way. He's gen - tle, he is kind; I'll nev - er, ev - er find a

bet - ter friend than old dog Tray.

1,2   3

2. The
3. When

Old King Cole

16th Century English Song

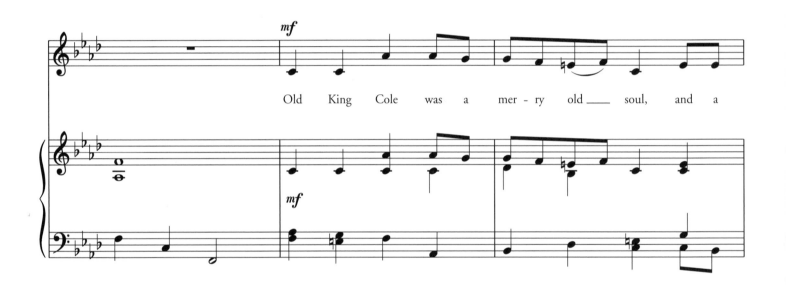

Old King Cole was a mer-ry old ___ soul, and a

mer-ry old soul was he. He ___ called for his pipe, and he

Peace of the River

Glendora Gosling

Viola Wood
arranged by Benjamin M. Culli

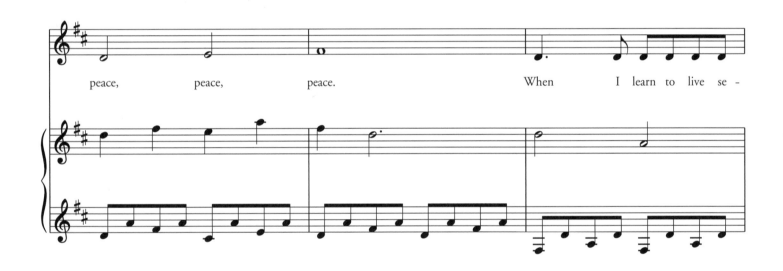

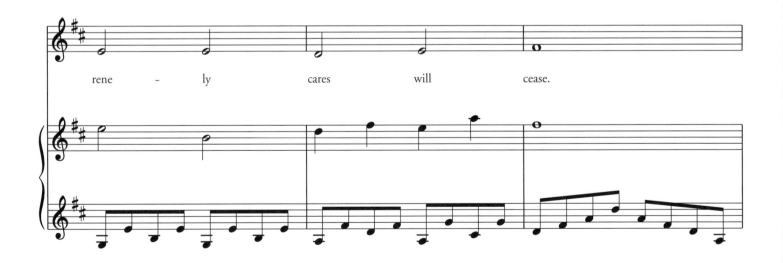

From the hills I gath-er cour - age, vi - sion of the day to be.

Strength to lead and faith to fol - low,

all are giv-en un-to me.

Peace I ask of thee, oh

poco rit.

riv - er, peace, peace, peace.

The Quest

Bohemian Folk Song

1. Why are you stand - ing out - side, young man? Come in and
2. We did not come here to rest our - selves, we came to
3. "John, dear, be care - ful and do not choose one who is
4. "John, dear, be care - ful and do not choose one who can't

tell us your quest; _____ and if you're feel - ing a
stand up and woo. _____ Three charm - ing daugh - ters we
proud to the core, _____ for she would not take a
smile or look bright, _____ for she might scowl at you

bit fa - tigued, sit down and talk while you
know you have, we wish to get one from
step with you, ev - en as far as the
ev - 'ry day, from ear - ly morn - ing till

Red River Valley

Traditional American Cowboy Song
arranged by Benjamin M. Culli

(Believed to be about the valley between
Oklahoma and Texas, or alternatively, about
the Red River of the North that flows from
Minnesota and the Dakotas to Lake Winnipeg.)

From this val - ley they say you are go - ing. _____ I will
Won't you think of this val - ley you're leav - ing _____ and how

miss your bright eyes and sweet smile, for they say you are tak - ing the
lone - ly and sad it will be; and __ think of the heart that you're

sun - shine _____ that has bright - ened our path - way a -
break - in' _____ and the grief that you are caus - in'

while.
me. } Come and sit by my side if you love me. _____ Do not

has - ten to bid me ad - ieu. Just re - mem - ber the Red Riv - er

Val - ley, _____ and the { girl } { boy } that has loved you so true.

The Sea Breeze

English words by
Hervey White

Folksong

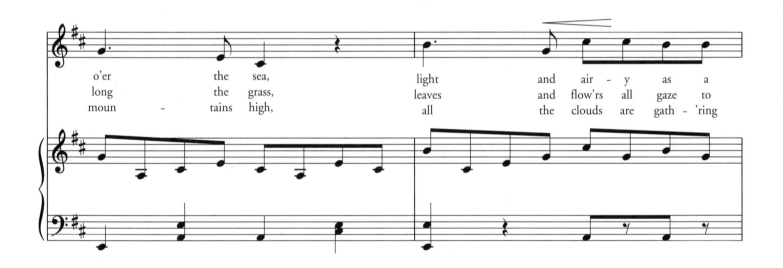

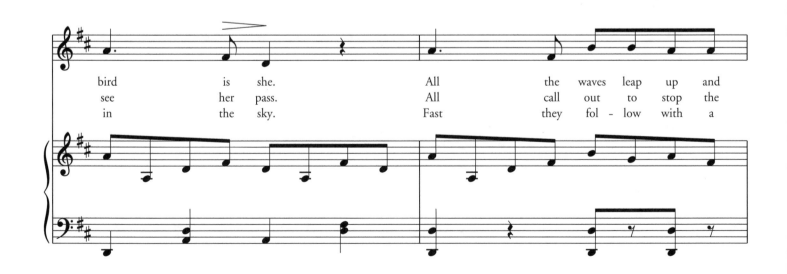

call in glee, "Ma - ri - a - ni - na, fly no
fleet - ing lass, "Ma - ri - a - ni - na, be a
mer - ry cry, "Ma - ri - a - ni - na, come from

more. Dance with us and all the more, be a wave and dance to
flow'r, dance with us through - out the hour, for we feel your mag - ic
far, why not stay right where you are, dance with us and be a

shore. Ma - ri - a - ni - na, Ma - ri - a -
pow'r. Ma - ri - a - ni - na, Ma - ri - a -
star. Ma - ri - a - ni - na, Ma - ri - a -

ni - na, be a wave and dance for - ev - er more."
ni - na, dance with us, and be a lit - tle flow'r."
ni - na, dance with us, a twin - kling, glanc - ing star."

Sidewalks of New York

Words and Music by
Charles B. Lawlor
and James W. Blake

we formed a mer - ry group.

Boys and girls to - geth - er,

we would sing _____ and waltz, _____ while

Ton - y played the or - gan on the

Sit Down, Sister

African-American Spiritual
arranged by Benjamin M. Culli

Oh, won't you sit down? Lord, I can't sit down. Oh, won't you

sit down? Lord, I can't sit down. Oh, won't you sit down? Lord, I

can't sit down, 'cause I just got to heav-en. Goin' to look a-round.

Skip to My Lou

19th Century American Game Song

Lou,   Lou,   skip to my Lou,   Lou,   Lou,   skip to my Lou,

Lou,   Lou,   skip to my Lou,   skip to my Lou, my dar - ling.

1. Lost my part - ner, what'll I do? Lost my part - ner, what'll I do?
2. I'll find an - oth - er one pret - ti - er than you, I'll find an - oth - er one pret - ti - er than you,
3. Flies in the but - ter - milk, shoo, shoo, shoo. Flies in the but - ter - milk, shoo, shoo, shoo.

Lost my part - ner, what'll I do?
I'll find an - oth - er one pret - ti - er than you, Skip to my Lou, my dar - ling.
Flies in the but - ter - milk, shoo, shoo, shoo.

Lou, Lou, skip to my Lou, Lou, Lou, skip to my Lou,

Lou, Lou, skip to my Lou, skip to my Lou, my dar - ling. dar - ling.

Sleep, Baby, Sleep

Folksong

Softly Sleeping

Franz Schubert

Slowly

Soft - ly sleep - ing,
Slum - ber, slum - ber,

my be - lov - ed treas - ure, gen - tly rocked __ by moth-er's lov - ing hand.
in thy down - y __ cra - dle, moth - er soft - ly sings a lul - la - by.

Rest, and peace - ful, hap - py dream - ing may you find ___ in
Soon you'll wak - en, warm ___ and ro - sy, when the sun ___ is

pleas-ant slum - ber - land.
shin-ing in __ the __ sky.

Some Folks

Stephen Foster

1. Some folks like to sigh, some folks do, some folks do.
2. Some folks fear to smile, some folks do, some folks do.
3. Some folks fret and scold, some folks do, some folks do. They'll
4. Some folks get gray hairs, some folks do, some folks do.
5. Some folks toil and save, some folks do, some folks do. To

Some folks long to die, but that's not me nor you.
Oth - ers laugh through guile, but that's not me nor you.
soon be dead and cold, but that's not me nor you.
Brood - ing o'er their cares, but that's not me nor you.
buy them - selves a grave, but that's not me nor you.

Long live the mer-ry, mer-ry heart that laughs by night and day, like the

Queen of Mirth, no mat-ter what some folks say.

Sweet and Low

Alfred Tennyson

Joseph Barnby

1. Sweet and low, sweet and low, wind of the west-ern
2. Sleep and rest, sweet sleep and rest, Fa - ther will come to thee

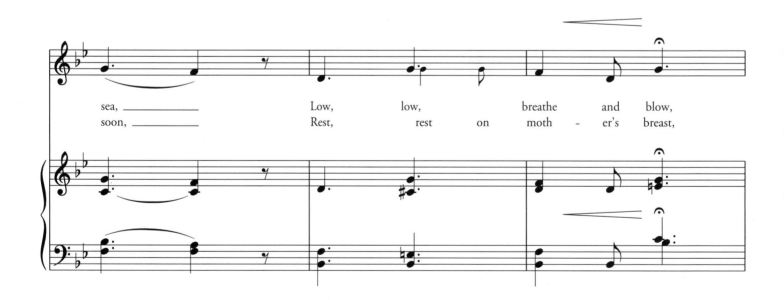

sea, _____ Low, low, breathe and blow,
soon, _____ Rest, rest on moth - er's breast,

wind of the west - ern sea. _____ O - ver the roll - ing
Fa - ther will come to thee soon. _____ Fa - ther will come to his

wa - ters go, come from the dy - ing moon _____ and blow,
babe in the nest, sil - ver sails _____ all out of the west,

blow him a - gain to me, _____ While my lit - tle one,
un - der the sil - ver moon. _____ Sleep, my lit - tle one,

while my pret - ty one sleeps. _____
sleep, my pret - ty one, sleep. _____

Tell Me Why

Traditional American Folksong
arranged by Benjamin M. Culli

Smoothly, with an easy flow

Oh, tell me why the stars do shine. Oh, tell me why the i - vy twines. Oh,

cause God made the stars to shine, be - cause God made the i - vy twine, be -

Spinning Song

German Folk Song

"Spin, my be – lov – ed daugh – ter new shoes for your feet!"

"No, no, my dear – est moth – er, I'm feel – ing de – feat."

"Spin, my be – lov – ed daugh – ter, I'll buy you a dress."

"No, no, my dear – est moth – er, I on – ly need rest."

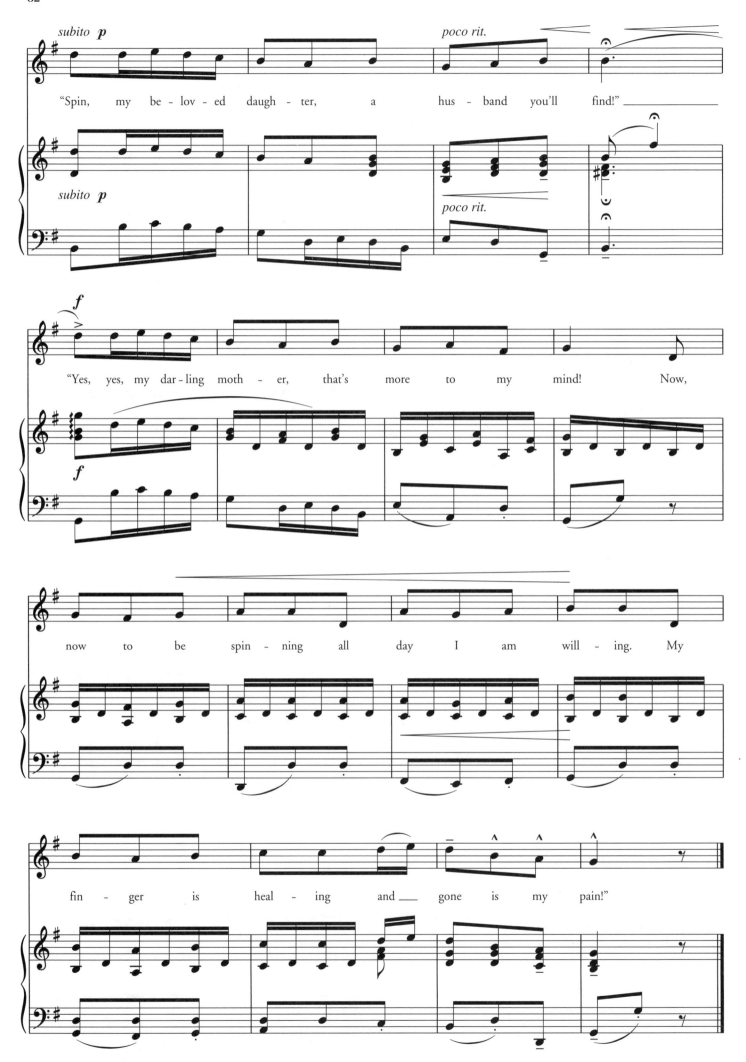

Toyland

Glen McDonough

Victor Herbert

Slowly and dreamily

When you've grown up, my dears, _____ and are as old as I, _____ you'll of-ten pon-der on the years that roll so swift-ly by, my dears, that roll so swift-ly

Lit - tle girl and boy - land, while you dwell with - in it _____ you are

ev - er hap - py then. Child - hood's Joy - land,

mys - tic, mer - ry Toy - land! Once you pass its

bor - ders you can ne'er ___ re - turn a - gain. _____

The Weather

American Folksong
arranged by Benjamin M. Culli

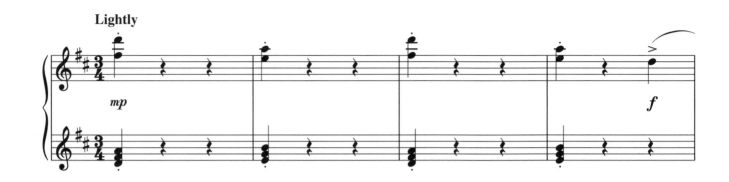

never feels hot and he never feels cold, be -
neith - er the cold nor the heat ev - er felt, be -
calls for at least three full suits at a time; a

cause where he lives sum - mer nev - er oc - curs, and the
cause in the win - ter his sum - mers be - gin, and the
thick one and thin one for days cold and hot, and a

rest of the year he wears plen - ty of furs. ⎞
rest of the year he wears croc - o - dile skin. ⎬ Too - ra -
me - di - um weight for the days that are not. ⎠

mf

lee, _____ Too - ra - lay, _____ ⎧ And the
⎨ And the
⎩ And a